# Science in Our Lives

by Ann Howard

# How does technology affect our lives?

## Finding New Ways

People always want to know how things work. As people learn things, they get new ideas. People invent tools to help. A **tool** helps people do work more easily or in a new way. This means people use technology. **Technology** is using knowledge to design new tools and new ways to do things. Tools can be simple or complicated.

Arches were an important invention in ancient Rome. An **invention** is something made for the first time. The Romans needed water for their cities. They learned that arches with a central stone could hold heavy things. They used these arches to make bridges. Bridges were used to move water to the cities.

The keystone, or central stone wedged at the top, keeps the stones of the arch in place.

## Technology in Your Home

Your home is made up of many parts. These parts form systems. The systems must work together.

What happens when you flush the toilet? You use the plumbing system. This system is made of faucets, drains, sinks, and pipes. These parts all work together.

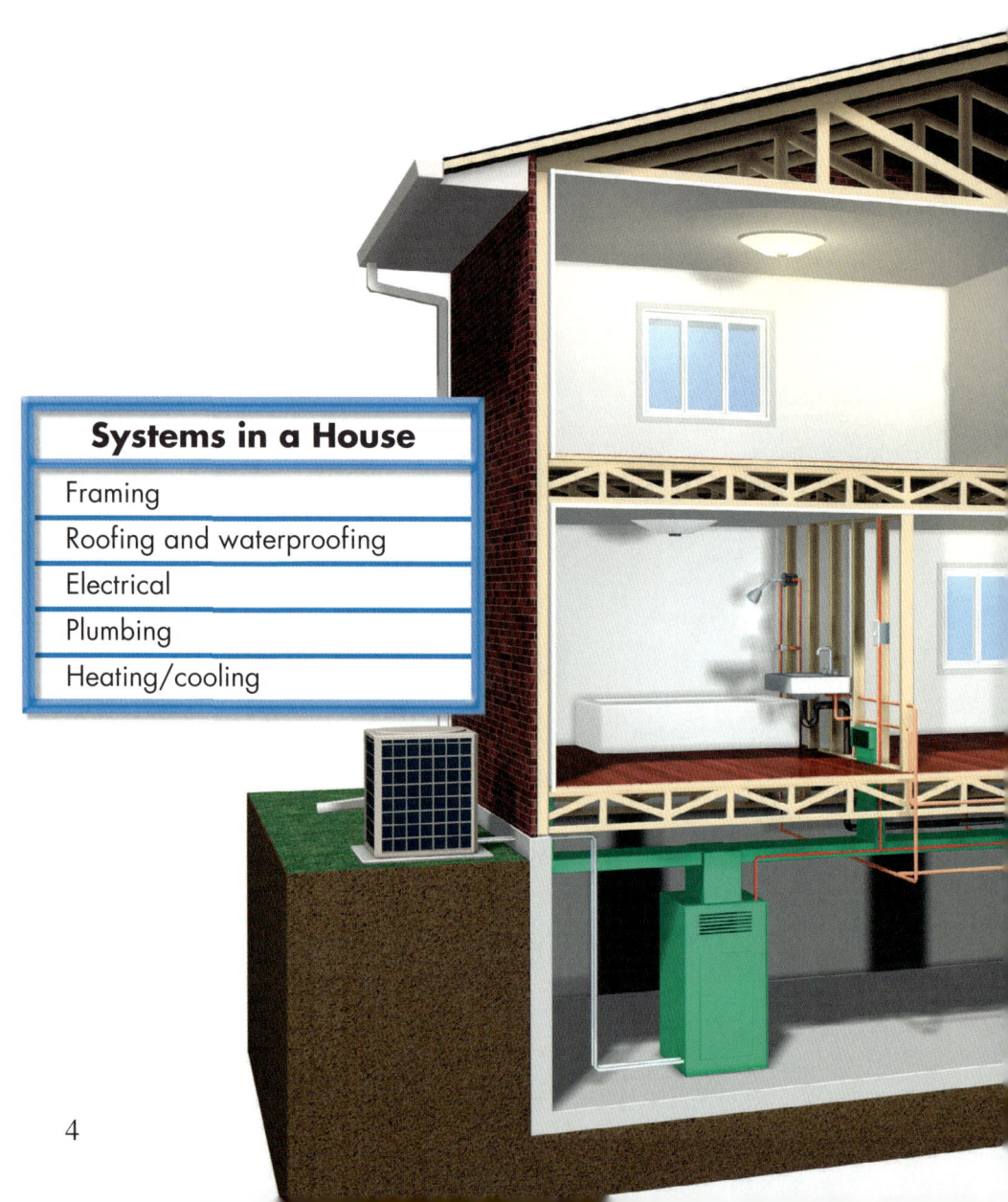

| Systems in a House |
|---|
| Framing |
| Roofing and waterproofing |
| Electrical |
| Plumbing |
| Heating/cooling |

Some water in the plumbing system goes through a heater. The electrical system is linked to it. Electricity heats the water. Together, the plumbing and electrical systems make it possible for you to take a hot shower.

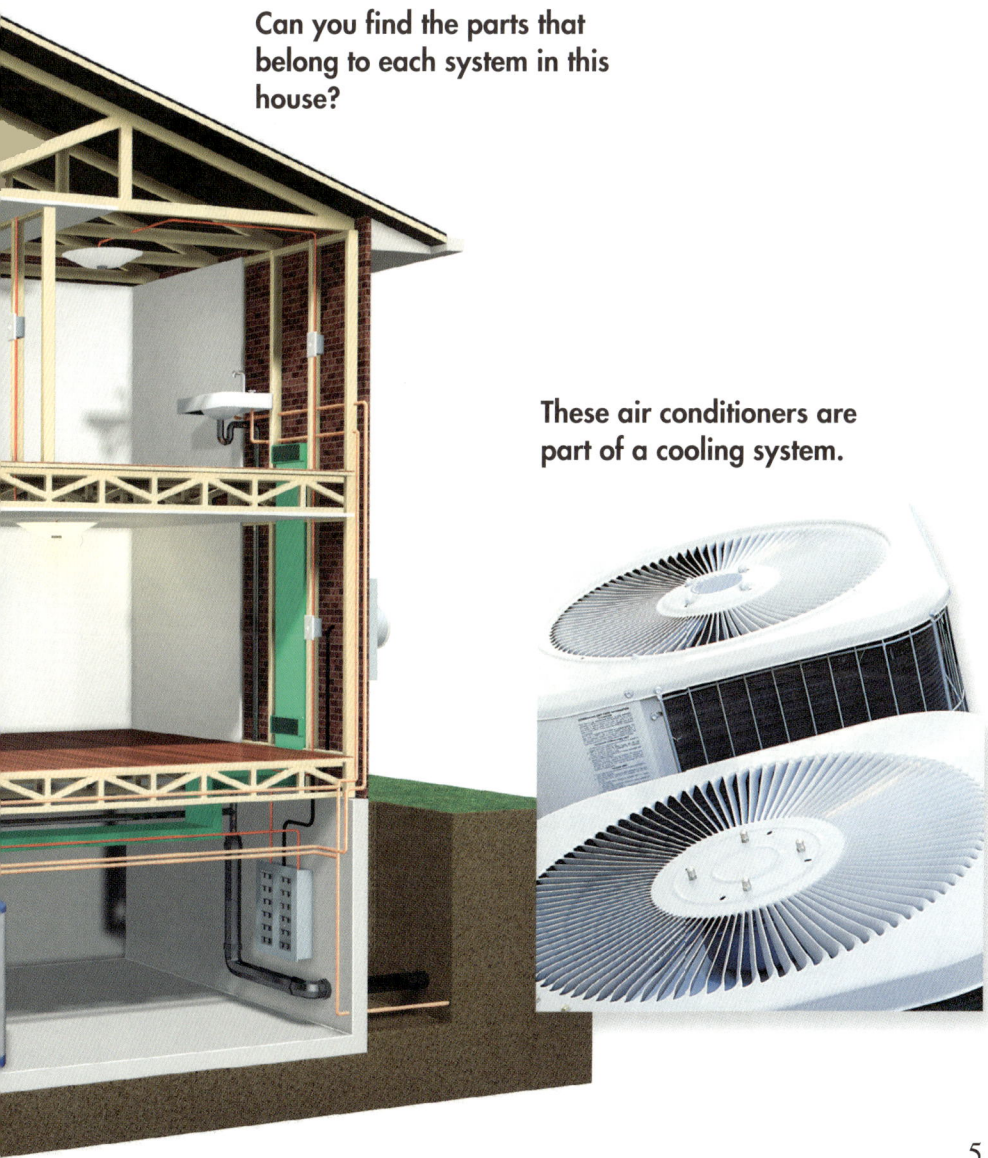

Can you find the parts that belong to each system in this house?

These air conditioners are part of a cooling system.

How is a house built? Technology is used from the beginning. Boards are placed in very special ways. Builders know where to place boards to make a house strong. Each part must be put in the right place to make a strong frame. This is why planning is important.

Particle boards are used in walls. The boards are made of wood chips. Such wood chips used to be burned. When burned, they caused pollution. New technology turns those chips into strong boards that are used in walls.

Wood chips are pressed and glued together to make particle boards.

## Technology Yesterday, Today, and Tomorrow

Two hundred years ago, kitchens did not have electricity. There was no refrigerator. People had to burn wood in a stove to cook food. Cooking meals could take all day.

People began inventing new things. First, ice boxes were used to keep food cold. Then, electric refrigerators replaced ice boxes. Today, microwave ovens cook food in seconds. Electric dishwashers wash dishes for you.

Airtight seals for plastic bowls were invented in 1947.

The non-stick coating on this pan was invented in 1954.

In the past, people played records to listen to music. As a record spun, a metal needle moved along the grooves of the record. Then a machine turned the vibrations from the needle into music. Today's DVD players use light beams to read the information on computer-coded plastic discs. Then a computer changes the information from the discs into images on a screen.

Some people think that computers will run your entire home in the future. A refrigerator may be able to order food when it becomes empty. Technology may make this possible.

Both CD and DVD players use light beams. The light beams play back the music and movies on the discs.

# What are some new technologies?

## Tools for Extending Our Senses

Sailors once used math and the stars to find their way. Now they can use a Global Positioning System (GPS). This system uses space satellites. The satellites send signals. A ship's GPS computer uses the signals like a map. Many cars today have a GPS.

Satellites can be used in many other ways. Forecasters use pictures taken by satellites to predict the weather.

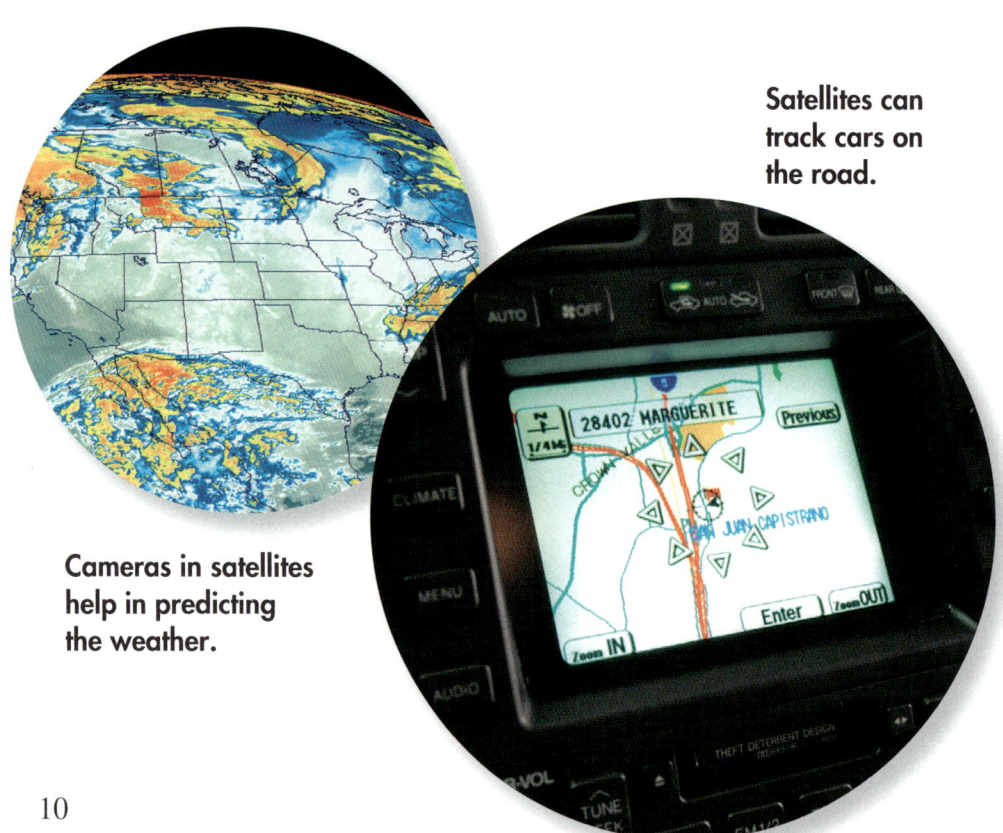

Cameras in satellites help in predicting the weather.

Satellites can track cars on the road.

## Tools for Processing Information

A **computer** stores, processes, and sends electronic information very fast! Computer technology is all around you. Computer chips are found in digital watches, cameras, and even cars.

Optical fibers are making computers better. These fibers are strands of bendable glass that carry light. The fibers are replacing copper wires in computer and telephone systems. Optical fibers do not get hot, as wires do. They also take up less space than wires. They can even carry much more information.

Optical fibers (right) are used in communication systems now instead of copper wires (left).

Changing to new fiber optic technology requires a lot of work.

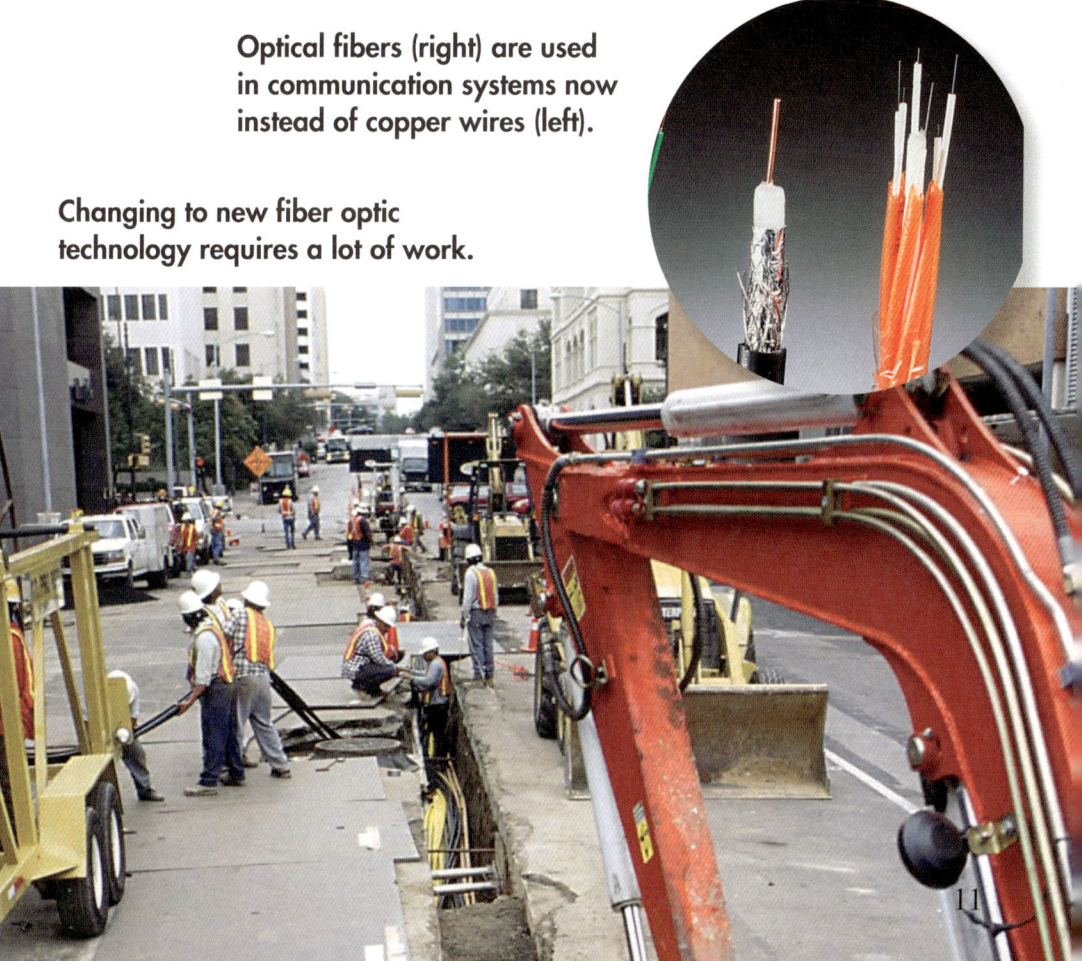

Highway engineers design roads such as the ones pictured above.

Highways were first built in the United States so military vehicles could move quickly.

## Tools for Transporting Materials

Roads are important to us. We use them to get to school and to work. We use them to transport goods. We use them to visit friends and family.

The National Highway System is made up of over 160,000 miles of highways. These highways go between the states in our country. About 80 million trucks haul supplies on these highways. About 120 million cars move people from place to place.

Roads are not the only way of moving people and things. People and freight are moved using trains and planes too.

But rivers were the first transportation system in the United States. Rivers are still full of boats moving goods today. Technology will always keep things moving!

## Unexpected Uses

Technology uses are not always planned. The microwave oven is a good example. In 1946 Percy Spencer was working to improve radar. He was testing a light bulb. The bulb used microwave energy.

One day, Spencer stood by the tube. A candy bar in his pocket melted. Spencer then placed popcorn kernels near the microwave energy. They popped. Spencer discovered that microwaves could cook foods fast! Soon, the microwave oven was invented.

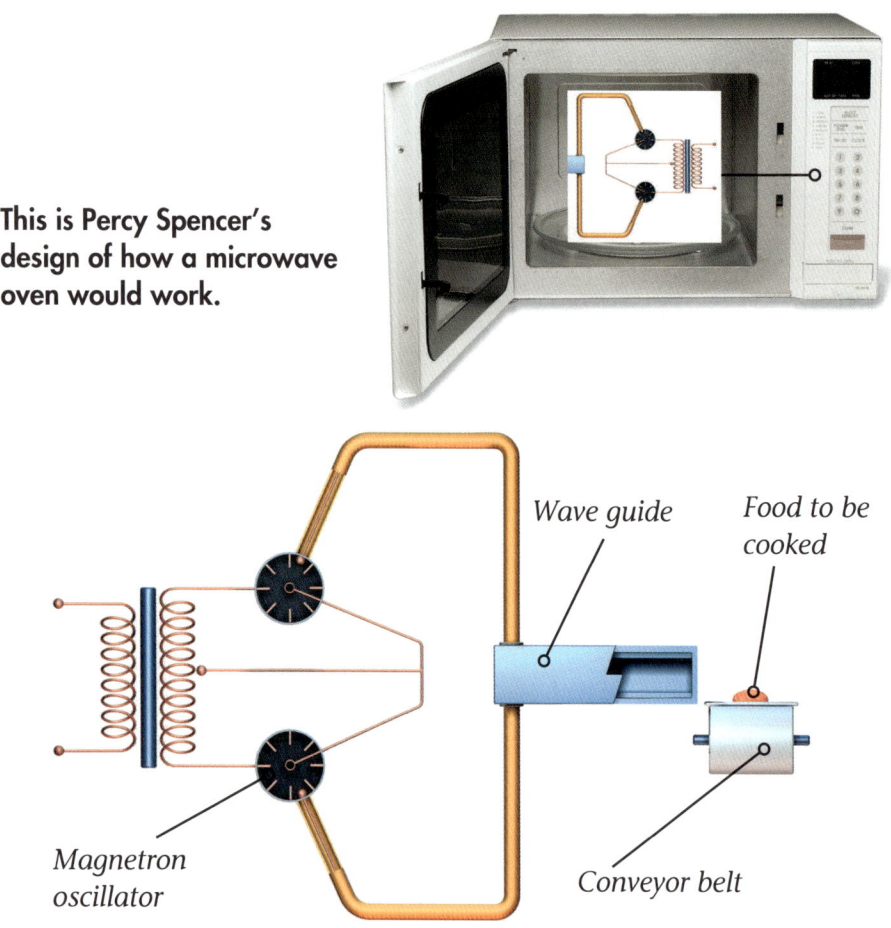

This is Percy Spencer's design of how a microwave oven would work.

*Wave guide*

*Food to be cooked*

*Magnetron oscillator*

*Conveyor belt*

Do you watch TV? Glass tubes were used to show the picture in early television sets and computers. But these tubes were big and heavy. With new technology, screens are light in weight. The LCD screen was invented in 1970 by James Fergason. LCD stands for liquid crystal display. Liquid crystals control the flow of light. This makes an image on the screen. These screens do not need heavy glass tubes. They are also flat in shape. So they take up less space.

**Flat LCD screens take up less space than older glass screens.**

# How does technology help us get energy?

## Using Energy

Put in a DVD. Heat up a snack in the microwave. Just be sure everything is plugged in! None of this would be possible without electricity.

Before electricity, people used energy from wind and water. Water-powered mills were built near rivers. The force of flowing water turned a wheel. At a sawmill, the wheel turned rods, gears, and belts. This powered saws that cut wood.

Windmills were also used to do work. Windmills use wind for power. Turning blades move gears in a box. Energy in the gears moves a rod up and down. This can be used to pump water from under the ground.

There are good and bad things about using windmills and water mills. Both wind and water are renewable sources of energy. They do not cause pollution. But they don't make enough power for all our needs.

**Windmills use wind to pump water.**

## Producing Electricity

Waterwheel technology is still used in hydroelectric power dams. These dams are built on rivers. Water in lakes behind the dams stores potential energy. To free this energy, gates let water into a power station. The flowing water spins the blades of a waterwheel in a turbine. The kinetic energy of water is changed into electricity in a generator. People use the electricity for power.

This generator can change the kinetic energy of flowing water into electricity.

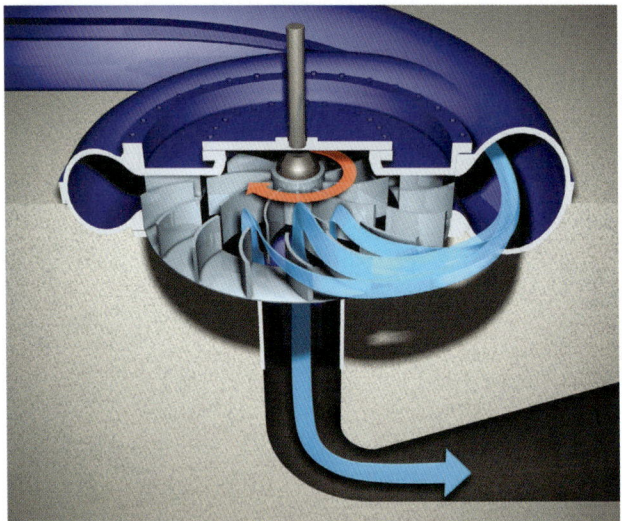

Connected to each generator is a turbine. The energy of moving water spins the blades in the turbine.

Hydroelectric power does not make much pollution. But the lakes behind dams can cause flooding.

There are other ways to make electricity. One way is by burning coal, oil, or natural gas. The heat created is used to boil water. The boiling water makes steam. Pressure from the steam turns wheels in electricity generators.

This technology makes plenty of electricity. But it also creates the problem of air pollution.

**Hoover Dam is one of the largest dams in the world.**

## Future Sources of Energy

Our need for energy keeps growing. How will we keep meeting this need?

Solar energy may be one answer. This energy comes from sunlight. Special panels collect sunlight. Each panel has lots of small solar cells. They change energy from the Sun into electricity. Solar energy is common in deserts. The Sun shines there much of the time.

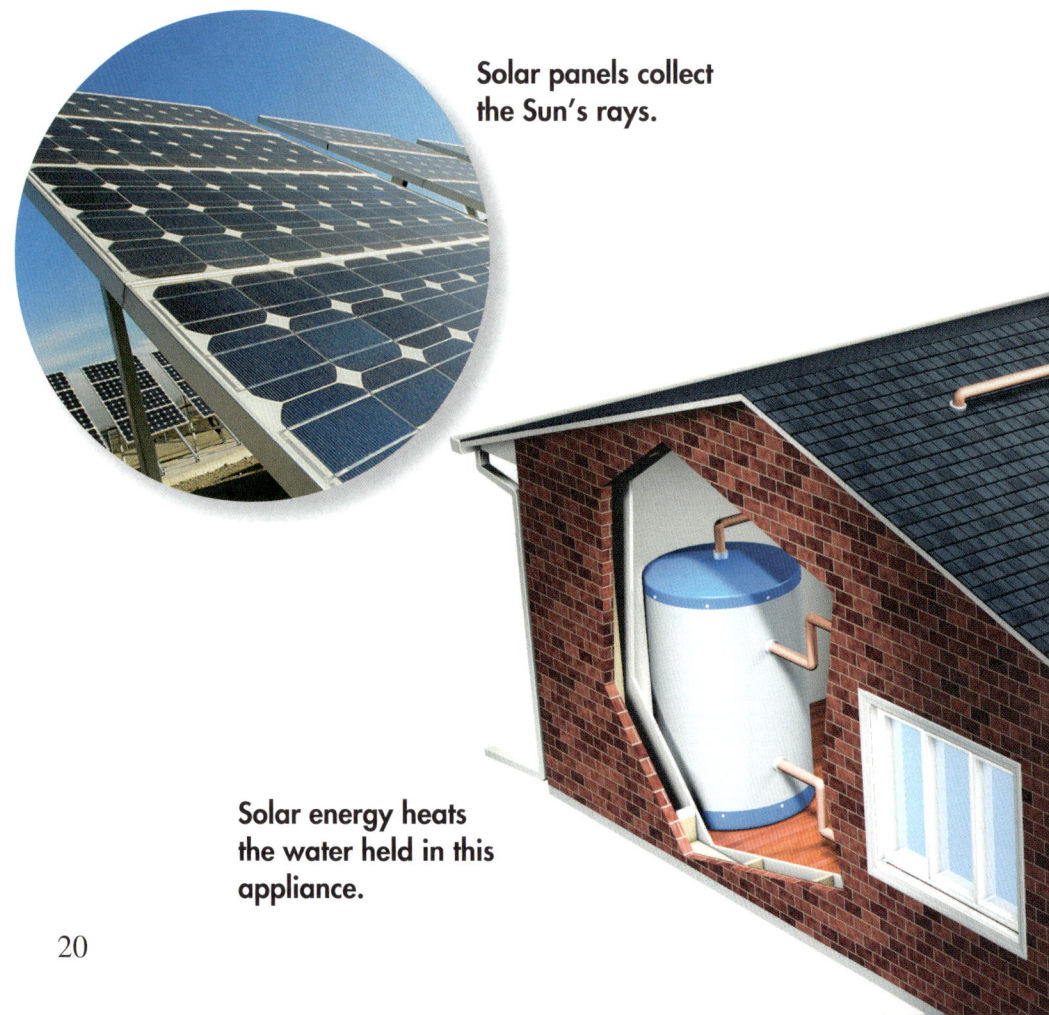

Solar panels collect the Sun's rays.

Solar energy heats the water held in this appliance.

Thanks to new technology, solar energy costs less. People can buy panels to put on their roofs. But these panels make hot water, not electricity.

Here's how it works. First, water runs through small tubes. Next, the Sun's rays are changed into heat. This happens when the panels absorb the rays. Then the heat warms the water in the tubes. Finally, the hot water flows into a tank. It is stored until it is used.

Wind energy is helping too. Windmills are put in places that get strong winds. Huge blades change the kinetic energy of wind into electrical energy.

Computers are used to tell when wind conditions have changed. Motors then adjust the direction and angle of the blades. This way, electricity is made whenever strong winds blow.

**Windmill blade wheels can be wider than a football field is long!**

Technology makes new ways of creating electricity possible. It also helps the systems in your home to work together. Technology helps us every day. It has changed our lives in many ways. Who knows how technology will change our lives in the future.

## Glossary

**computer**     a machine that stores, processes, and sends electronic information quickly

**invention**     something made for the first time

**technology**     the use of knowledge to make new tools and new ways to do things

**tool**     something that helps people do work more easily